CXXXVI

lived in its entirety
or otherwise by

joseph KENYON IV

composed during our
modern orbit schedule of

MMVI — MMXVI

edition **I**, *published* **V.MMXVI**

for
KIV

95
CINE

◀ "CXXXVI" Ⓡ (2016) A man comes to discover his brain has shattered, and attempts to go back in time to reverse the charges. Joe Kenyon IV, Christopher Walken appear. (1 hr 29 min) *cinemax* ★★

written in & inspired by

UNION, MIDDLESEX. MONMOUTH
New Jersey
& CAPE MAY COUNTIES

BUCKS & MONTGOMERY
PENNSYLVANIA
COUNTIES

Ⓜ Manhattan & Brooklyn Ⓙ
New York City

① ALL THRU
Australia

INVENTORY

MMVI–MMXVI

PROCESSION

"Peace™ be with you."

"And also with you!"

Assume positions.

~

Greetings from the Chemical Coast.

There would be an evil, friendly gargoyle standing guard, every single day just the same, as I'd find my way home through streets of university names.

I always wondered who Stiles was.

Manifested holidays, he stayed for quite a few years, probably not doing much else but scaring the cats and feeding the squirrels. But he did his job.

i.
JAZZ & CIGARETTES

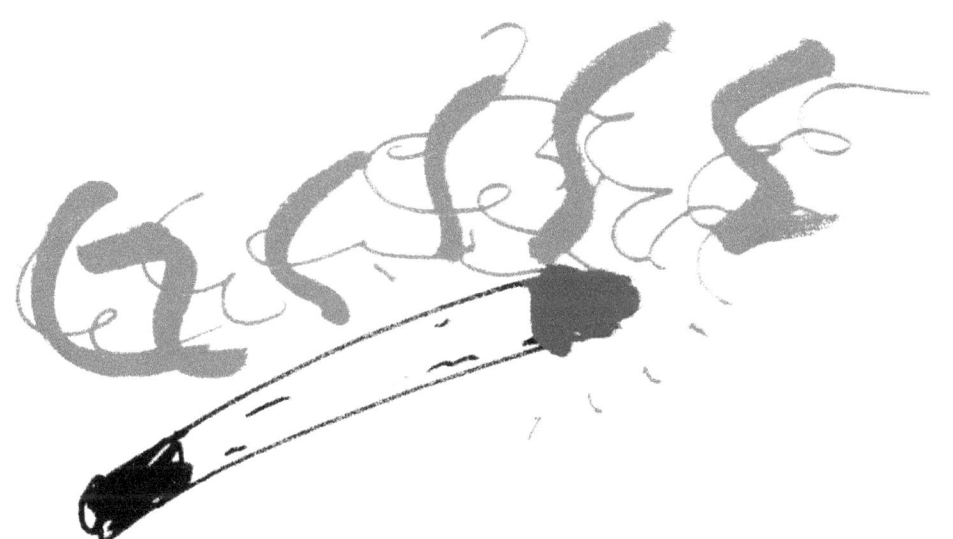

THRU TRAFFIC
NEXT EXIT 5 MILES

EXIT **11**

GARDEN STATE

PARKWAY ↗

Woodbridge

In his 1966 essay *"Plumons l'Oiseau"* (*"Let's Pluck the Bird"*), author Hervé Bazin proposed a handful of innovative, yet seldom-used punctuation marks; One of which being the *point d'amour* (the *"love point"*).

ORANGE TUNNELS

I've seen orange tunnels
ever since I was a child.
They brought out the best in me.
I've known orange tunnels
ever since I was a kid,
like I've known chills down my spine,
and epic moments in time.

JAZZ & CIGARETTES

Jazz loves cigarettes
The two make love in so many ways
The juice, feuding and fueling
the straying imagination
of the conduit,
doing his best to let go and do nothing
as each strike of the piano key
tries to speak everything
the jazzman can't.

I'm the jazzman,
and the ink in this fancy pen
is the nicotine fueling me
to release myself onto the paper,
and tell you things in a way
I know pretty well,
believe it or not.

GOOD DAYS

It shines through in the wrinkles of your face
taking them down, one by one
it shows you the smile you've been waiting for
under everyone else's sun
but it proves to you once and for all
the bad is just part of the fun

REO

withered waitress
three blocks from Bergen Street
plugs in and understands
the first look of the night to come
it may end up being rough
on diner clock til dawn of sun
haggard voice'll ask you,
            "How you doin, hun?"
keep the small-talk going
til you gotta up n run
nightshift moving faster
for her til the dawn of sun
thankful for the tip you left her,
            "See ya later, hun..."

RED WINE

Red wine is
sexual tension
and deep thought
rolled together
like sushi.

JAZZ & CIGARETTES, *pt.II*

...I'm no jazzman
because if I were,
I'd be able to perfectly describe —
without a single filter —
where I want to bring you.

a NERVOUS WARMTH

A tinted square a sienna,
aided by the blinds,
the night, the streetlight,
with fuzzy eyesight.
Classical guitar in sync
with the moon, as a
jazzman is traded in.
Delirious and she's in here,
and wherever she
happens to be,
she's looking straight at me
with red wine in her eyes
so deep that she can hardly see

COLTON COURT

Gravel,
pink sand standing up
to verge of rain
but still the time
enjoyed as much,
would love
another game

SUNSET BEACH

The gravel,
hard on foot
and loud when
driven over,
fight with keys
and blast A.C.
indoors in
mid-October

EXIT 0
NORTH   TO
109   9
N Cape May
CAPE MAY-LEWES FERRY
1 MILE

FADING ROOTS

Go for your dreams,
but keep it realistic
Retain the naive,
but drop all the mystic
Trade the cool hair
for a tube of dull lipstick
Become the full cynic,
sedate the artistic

LOVESICK

break the curse to make it worse
before it all gets better
if she don't get you high no more,
might as well forget her

GRAY HAIR

And never did I know
until the night declared me wrong:
Eventually she got me back
by being in my song.

ii.
GOLDEN COAST

FIRST AWAKE

I love being the first awake,
and the last to go to sleep
I'm always afraid I'll miss something great
that I'd really love to see.
I'll set my alarm for just before dawn,
but I'll get up quarter to three
I love being the first one awake,
and the last to fall asleep.

4 : 1 5

4:15, birds are chirpin'
up all night on nothin' workin'
one day left to finish sortin'
can't believe it's fuckin' mornin'

EYRE HIGHWAY

Among the first
to experience golden sunrise
at the bay,
with waves few thousand
miles wide, ensuring separate day.
From Bondi Beach, across a desert
with hardly a word to say,
I can't believe, for the life of me,
that I don't remember your name.

CAUGHT *a* STARE

"Ever since the house party, I've been
catching a different vibe. Even the living
room looks different. Lighting makes
anything possib—
She shouldn't be looking at me like that."

TOUCH

"Like trombones and tympanis and all the
other things in the band room that no one
wants to carry, there's no going back now;
I've been summoned to get started on
excuses. But first..."

I WANT *to* TAKE *a* TRIP...

Lavender holly leaves
on blue grass
under purple sky
with red wine
while it's
cutting through the tunnels

1 PACIFIC HWY

Gold Coast 59
Ballina 191
Sydney 978

ELLA'S STAYING
in SYDNEY...

Ella was young and into me,
and I was too young for anybody
Too immature to be distracted,
child-like, but old I acted.
Distracted by the substance of
adolescence, brought about
way, way too soon.
She told me on the hotel stairs,
kinda tried to care but
that poor girl,
as adorable as she was,
had hollered up to
a window that had not yet
opened up...
A handful of years,
just fighting for a ladder.

Ella's father died a year later
on September 11th, but by then,
there was already hardly any
correspondence sent.

CHANNEL 78

(an adult-oriented haiku)

Sneaky grandfather
and scrambled television;
good ol' Spice channel

WINDOW CLIMB

creaks are coming
from upstairs,
sneaking into
bedroom lair,
convert attic
moonlit floor,
visit hours
twelve to four.
cuttin' short on
certain nights,
wide awake but
shut the lights.
and if she wants to
visit me,
a window climb
for company...
cable vine serves
ladder sense,
follow glowing
TV sets.
between the two
escaping views
play lullabies and
night-light tunes.

EXIT 117

35 36

Keyport
Hazlet
1 MILE

ROUTE 36

The Sun had always gotten through to me,
no matter the time of day.
I was lucky enough to
receive all the rays
as a child...
Years later, I end up crazily happy
and happily crazy, a few blocks from
that long stretch of road that connected
normalcy to summertime;
Lord knew that sunburn was unreal.
It was a short tease of an indefinite warmth...
Better off that way, I feel.

I could have wandered those roads
'til my feet fell off, and I'd have loved
every second of it.
No matter how blistered I'd be in the end,
I'd gladly walk off all the pain of it.

CHANNEL 96

Three digits –
3, 9, 5 –
will cost a lonely five spot
and a couple hours time.
Endless scrolling banter
yet his choice remains the same;
All he wants to do is hear
his song selection played.
Equivalence of barroom jukes
will charge the kid his week,
traded chores, allowance gone,
but still the song he seeks.

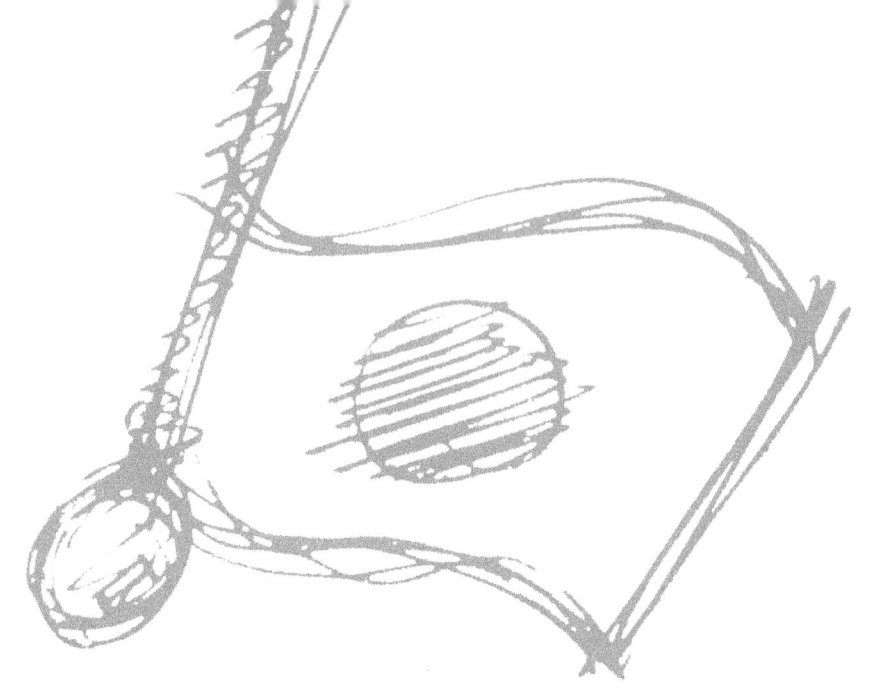

the SPIRITUAL

I'm not sure what happened to them, but the story
so small inspires nonetheless. The best is only
heard inside your head. Keys of Japan made their
way through the postal system, collaged with
stamps, supplying generosity and ideas, reminders
and melody.

POOLSIDE 609

A smashed mouth or three,
thanks to painted separation of
hot concrete and chlorine sea.
Sunken headgear found
in midday waters,
nine   feet   deep.
Seems much bigger, as
Amherst hoodlums
break the slide again,
guilty pleasures set the stage
for summer vacation.

'99

(haiku for the millennium **MM***)*

we lost zero light,
banged pots and pans like normal,
then we went to sleep.

iii.

NO BUSINESS HERE

FRESHMAN

(a fourth grade haiku)

sunglasses bound
an evil Mr. Pickton
on a sports game show

SOPHOMORE

    I still have the first real mixtape I was ever given, twelve years later glad she made a CD to go with it.

    I still remember the songs, I can tell you the artists, I can sing back the lyrics, I can tell you the color ink. She grew up down the block then moved but we sat next to each other in math class, when I was so stoned I couldn't answer teacher fast, no I didn't pass.

    Not my fault entirely, the guy had spoke so thick, that by the end of class I'm tired.

CHANNEL 36

Senior year, I had the bright idea
since we had access to the
city's television station right inside
our video production class
to play some filthy trash on glass
for all the town to see,
as channels flickered quickly past;
I kept the plan to me.
I cannot recommend, condone,
endorse you if you try,
I cannot be considered guilty
if I should inspire...
But if I shared ideas and got
some friends, we'd all succeed,
Five years late on switching
old cassettes for DVDs...

JUNIOR

the best teachers
were the worst
and vice versa
I realize that now
as they realize
their kids ain't
no better than I.

SENIOR

Sometimes I would show up
at two in the afternoon,
because I had no business there.
I didn't really bear a care,
I knew I had no business there.

Twice allotted absent days,
call in sick and lie and laze...
High school couldn't move too fast,
didn't think I'd even pass,
didn't even know my class,
it's my business, and I didn't
belong
there.

Say I'm Father, get some pity,
deepened voice that year I'm given;
Secretary down the street
had no idea it wasn't him.

(continued)
    We were told to come up with
    the greatest invention,
    twelfth year English, stupid lesson,
    I said music, warm reception;
    Girl that followed, no suspension,
    nice ovation, much frustration.
    "Microwave," she blurted out
    with hardly any hesitation;
    Dreamt a sudden flash of my
    expulsion and incarceration,
    stemming from a strangulation,
    resting home, a dream vacation.

    Never showed, and never showed,
    three gym classes senior year,
    and I never showed,
    and never showed,
    twenty days out by end September.
    Truant officer may remember.

    I was playing Mortal Kombat at the
    Chinese restaurant the next block over.

(continued)

   I'd never appear for detention,
   never ready to perform,
   instead I'd show up half-way through
   and walk right out the blue gym doors.
   Saturday, a room with no
   A/C at schoolweek's end,
   I'd show up after ten and walk
   right out the gym again.

Aside from the standard lunchroom brawl and the
occasional collaterally-damaged stray bottle cap,
I spent the entirety of my educational existence
thinking, and believing,

               "I have no business here."

(continued)
That same English class
held a few just short of
schoolboy trash,
morons fell for summer reading,
saw the plusses, rather sleeping.
I read Carlin,
reported on it,
was heckled on it,
teacher can fucking sit on it,
I'm the one with the book now,
you sit and listen to me...
Put me on that summer reading list,
and tell me how it feels
as my name comes through their teeth,
as you're introduced
to me.

iv.
the GRASPING HANDS *of*
POSSIBILITY

EARTH'S BEST KEPT SECRET

I hardly had a chance to even comprehend
your eyes that have that stare to them
that would make all your friends jealous
and you'd never even know
Don't worry about misunderstanding,
those weeks were few,
stare back in this direction again
I'm sorry, I couldn't understand...

of ARIES & AQUARIUS
The notion of her with someone else
comes true as everything fails

y o u r MORPHING MINDSET

Obtain the ability to set the line
Devising a solid scheme differs
from planning way too far ahead
Never let them mistake jokes
for genuine stupidity
Putting trivial matters on pedestals
and burying big pictures in the soil
does nothing but bring forth
forgotten potential
But without matter,
with the way I am built,
it feels like I'm trying to try
and since I can't, I beg you
to stop this wandering mind.

MISS TELEVISION INTELLIGENCE

Trading effort and will
to view the world from a screen,
echoes of wasted chances are heard
screaming as the zero risks taken
have thrown them over the edge regardless:
"Half the time, reality's something
not worth seeing."

SUMMER

bassline of summer is persistent,
reminiscent of a Misfire,
back deck with purple glow of a
short-lasting bookend of daylight.
what you can't capture tonight
will be remembered tomorrow,
warm sidewalks for those
without protection from what's
grossly passed over.
firework beats,
four per lighter flick,
snapping along with the band,
acoustics in hand,
harmonies we attempted for years.
now, I built a wall
of television screens,
to replay all the memories
back in thirty-five millimeter
negative streams...

INTERPLANETARY JESTER

with a fighting smile,
he juggles your demons
and skeletons under
eclipses he painted himself,
letting them dance in pitch dark
while fighting a tear on stage.

KARMA *in* REMISSION
It was then I had realized
that karma ain't comin',
no guns goin' off,
but a whole lotta runnin'.

ENDLESS, EMPTY DAYS
no matter how you try and try
they never fail to come to mind
a world where hearts anew may lie
foreign objects in the sky
hourglass not up nor down,
endless days go round and round

HARDLY *a* PLACE *of* HONOR

Losing my reactions and concerns,
I drag aimlessly on
and each step is a split road
Each turn back an entrance to a maze
I stumble at my own will
to try and grasp a sense of being
Now knowing mere confusion,
I want to feel

the GRASPING HANDS *of* POSSIBILITY

When morale is low and misery sets in,
learn to listen for specific voices
and through rigorous trial and error,
when experiments test successful,
The Transmissions
operating on a frequency all their own
broadcast their message…
Love the power you hold in your hands

ALIEN REMINDER:
Operating in reality
and making realistic decisions
produces realistic results,
whether or not you think you
actually exist!

02/01/2003

The aftermoment, a lifetime to touch
but we can't locate you anywhere
in a million pieces you shouldn't be
when there's only one of you to me—
I know I have no choice
but to respect how stubborn you are,
and how high you needed to soar
with each breath feeling grateful for;
as grateful as you're stubborn,
wide the sky that you had left us for

C Ø S M Ø N A U T

"The other side of history makes you wonder,
and the darkened sides of moons are sharing
one collective grin.
                    Who are you to tell me
                            what I choose to believe in?"

C O M M . C H E C K

in those seventeen,
let us be your safety net,
we got you if you trust us,
but we need you to believe...

I like to sit.

watching fireworks, on a ...

...burger at an absurd ... at 136.

cross of the legs and ... drew off 136, sitting bored, ...
lemmed, hardly enthused.

is roughly a mile a number ...
that much. I'd try it if I ...
... down with. Someone to ...
... home, Just 136.

... doing it all
... doing nothing
... kind a sitting

51

dissipating turns,
come to shout at strangers in a
so transparent, that you
don't tell in person.
smoke too many cigarettes, and think that
raising a brain so much will
a benefit, but
much candy is bad for you.
get through in time.
always maintain,
or later.
I know is what's intangible,
I can make it not.

do my box, 4/13/16

BOXED IN

52

of history

wonder and

of blue

a face.

moon really

have

to tell me what

Who are

just my think

we all know

love.

" " 4/10/16

BREAKING KAYABLE (prelude)

there's a

good

V.
BLACK MASK

WELCOME *to my* WORLD

(a haiku)

Welcome to my world!
I hope you enjoy your stay.
See you later, then!

BACK-UP BLESSINGS

(another haiku)

Make your own blessings
so when one finally dies,
you have a back-up

#9. HEALTH

I wrote down all my problems,
just like they say to do.
My health was number nine,
after work and money due.
I've been writing down my problems
for way too long it seems;
My health is number nine,
fuzzy medics tending dreams.
I've been writing down my problems,
ever since I've been alone...
My health is number nine,
reluctant claiming of my own.

My health's been number nine,
from the day that I begun
writing down my problems,
when it should be number one.

1 0 3 0 - *a*

Orange tunnels of light,
post-authority flare,
reach into your soul
staring out through smoke
at a Jersey sunrise
out a bedroom window.
This story seems so familiar,
I wonder if the paths I've never crossed
are wondering back just where I am.
I wonder who stood where I now stand.
Bring it back, something familiar…
Even if the faces remain the same
Though I never cared for this place,
I don't want to leave.
The same dirty mirror of mine
has shown a million faces of mine,
and it helps to bring it back.

SLACKER

I'm a slacker without even tryin'
Chemical Coastin', livin' and dyin'
raised too late, a lesson too short
I wish I had realized all this before
but if I could do it all over again,
would I stumble upon an identical end?
'cuz I still know what I don't know,
just like the rest of them.

Rahway ➡
Shore Pts ➡

SOMETHIN'

just a lil' somethin'
to ease all the growin'
i'm turnin' to nothin'
a devil is showin'

NO ATTENTION, PLEASE

Ducking under stress by way of smoke,
Make another mess just as a joke
I've said it all before
And I'd say it all again,
If you wouldn't cut me off right as I spo—

LETTERS UNREAD

Be my friend
Until the end,
Type your piece
But never send.
Be my friend
Until the end,
There is a game
I have to tend.
Be my friend
Until the end,
Private message
Marked unread
Be my friend
Until the end,
Real life is calling
down again.
Be my friend
Until the end,
I typed goodbye,
Forgot to send|

the BONES *of* ABRAHAM CLARK

and when you're leaving Rahway Park,
salute the bones of Abraham Clark,
uphill trespass on your mark,
restful quiet, Jersey dark
Neighbors and friends, a step downstream,
with every blizzard, every beam
committing theft of sweet serene,
veteran skeletons, shiny and clean

LIE

I joke so I can lie,
I lie so I can sleep,
I cannot sleep & stand,
But I can stand & lie, indeed

BLACK EYES

I messed with days that weren't mine
and never had to pay
'til once I woke with two black eyes
that never went away

in LIEU *of* INK

his heart through his hand
to the audient ten
in lieu of the ink
came blood from his pen
How's it that good
with vision askew
causes tenfold the grief
of a true bastard few?

FAKE *it* WELL

Stranger walking down the street
tells me I'm lookin' swell,
I turn too fast, my front falls off,
But I still fake it well.

#10. HEALTH

My health's been number nine
and would be until the end,
Until I checked my list and found
that my health is number ten.

HOPE
Wow, it worked!

PICK *your* POISON *2*

My poison's not as lethal
as you'd quite expect to be,
but believe me when I tell you that
it does just right for me

GHOSTS *of* FRIENDS

Every time you're slighted
by ghosts of friends no more,
each foot gains a gram,
I'm with you stompin'
through the floor

I GOT IT ALL, *pt. deux*

"I got it all", he said
sang within a stubborn head,
always livin' in the red
what he got, it made him dead.
"I had it all", he said
speaking softly from his bed,
rather hit the stage instead
fancy man, they called him Fred.

WRAPPED *in a* CONTINGENCY

wrapped in a contingency,
never a worry, only me
an ordinary emergency
a desperate need to slow it down,
allow myself to think,
and rearrange my mind as fast
as human eyes can blink.

REVERSE PATH

life imitates art,
when you're playing your own part
or you have an illusion to sell
you can tell a good story
manufacture the glory
and find misery in doing it well

life will start imitating art, self-sabotage
planting seeds for more misery to grow.

S U B W A Y   T R A I N

She had a bunch of cracks
in her hands that were kind of telling,
and fit the lighting of
a train station naturally.
She moved fast like a subway train,
and told me not to talk to
anyone talking to me.
Hardly ever straying
Jersey rails,
gripping metal poles with
neon green fingernails–
The center of me likes
watching it from outskirts,
because I can't catch all the
lights at once from
deep within its works...
How do we not know which way to go?
Not really from around here...

BETTER THINGS

(a haiku)

Writing a haiku
I have better things to do
with my fucking life

WAITING
A hundred lines of sight are fading,
A hundred army wives are waiting

I GOT IT ALL

"I got it all", she said
to herself inside her head,
as she tucked them into bed,
after they've been bathed and fed.
"I got it all", he said
as he placed another bet,
million bucks he'll surely net,
it's the worst I've seen him yet.
"I got it all", I said
to the doctor in my head,
as I got my fortune read,
"Son, be lucky you're not dead."

STICK *to my* GUNS

"Stick to your guns" was all I knew,
They got me screwed, they got me through.
Either way, I always drew.
The guns were mine, both tried and true.

STICK *to my* GUNS *II*

Stuck to guns I always knew,
They held me back, but I made do.
I played it safe and timing flew,
and always did I have a clue.

FALLEN *on* DEAF EARS

For every song that's written
there's a day that's gone unpaid,
and for every bullet bitten,
there's a lick that wasn't played.

RETIRED

i'll retire for a night,
and get up before the sun
to get so wrapped up in it all
just to retire again
i'm a boy at dawn
drop a pair by noon
an old man come evening,
retiring soon
my battles are broad
and some i won't fight,
but i'll bout with enemies
or friends every night.
i greeted a man
and offered my sword
and as he walks past,
a care nevermore
so then take my night
as it comes to an end,
i'll admit my defeat and
retire again

P E A C E L O R D

Do you have a dilemma yourself?
Seeking help to provide a solution?
I've developed some plans for
worldwide peace, but I'm
afraid you'll steal and misuse 'em...
I want my name on every little
paper, patent, receipt;
Copyright myself to death,
this peace belongs to me.
I'll trademark every postcard lost
like prisoners on their own,
because this peace is none of yours;
It's mine, and mine alone!

W O N T O N   S O U P

Little B can write a thousand
for my every three,
but I'm not sure that he can
blind recite his ABC's.
Ask him for a signature and
watch him try to sign,
a filthy, broken crayon
signs it different every time.

PICK *your* POISON

I wish the easier free-flow,
unpoisoned;
I wish the edge far gone,
yet so uneasy.
"We always maintain,"
like a monk's mantra,
repeatedly unapologetic.
I'll believe it in a day or two.
I wish the easier free-flow,
unburdened.
Give it a day or two...
I like my poison tamed
and almost harmless,
as I understand my friends
and what'll last until
until they're in bed.
I get it, I get it,
a bit too much and I'm into it,
Oh believe me, I understand.

Lincoln Tunnel
New York City

⬇   ⬇

BETTER THINGS #2

(yet another haiku)

Writing a haiku
Obviously, I don't have
better things to do

EXIT **127**

Woodbridge
Staten Island

NORTH

vi.
PEACE TALKS

à la CARTE

Layers of life
prepared à la carte,
you can down all the news
and the views that you want.
Angles and outlooks
are servings apart,
like finger food lessons
and slices of smarts.
Layered reality,
made à la carte,
comfort in flavors
like dreams in the dark.

SAFETY NETS

A safety net so strong, that
It's made with human flesh;
Growing stronger by the cell,
A web of living mesh—
And should one fall
to what would be an
ordinary death,
a chance for living safety nets
to catch a steady breath

WRITE *from the* DRUMS

don't tell anyone,
take it and run,
write from the drums
and spare you some fun

TEACHER

Sitting with yourself,
gathering thoughts
Playing crosses and naughts
Rebuilding your health
after battles you fought
Upon all your shelves,
the gold and unsought
Bask in the wealth
of the lessons you taught

KNOWLEDGE

No difference does the knowledge make,
when action breeds an old mistake;
You can't exist and not apply,
and live your life for knowing's sake.
An infant wrinkle in the brain
for every second you're awake
is useless when you can't connect
the knowledge to the point you make.

AHEAD *of the* PENDULUM

Taking the perspective from grounded
to grounded with benefits, so to speak.
I want to elevate my thoughts and
send them running to next week.
If nature's back and forth like elastic,
can you jump ahead of the curve,
pre-empting balance, how fantastic...
Shifting knowledge up a gear,
San Dimas-style, skip a year?
If you can understand your balance
like a clock's inner mechanics,
could you stabilize yourself
against a hurricane of panic?
...I don't think the crystal ball
can tell you what you oughta do,
but
I think that you
should start to think
a little
more
of you.

UPSTAIRS NEIGHBOR

The older man that lives upstairs,
the best we've ever had.
Even though he's loud as shit,
he ain't so fuckin' bad.
Kinda nice, a private man,
out at dawn and back by ten;
Wakes me up, but that's okay,
I go in early, anyway.

~

Now I'm pretty pissed since I'm
in need of time to breathe,
yet all I hear is creaking,
dude is gettin' more than me.

BOXED IN

Welcome to my box, that
of which I take good care;
Or at least the best attention
that your boy can bear to spare.
To breathe, I punch these tiny holes,
for six I'll put a pair;
but I find it just as comfy
with my own supply of air.

the CHASE, DESCRIBED

I like the vibe you're putting out
so we're gonna expand on it
and make it our own
and see where we can bring it,
and where it can bring us
these are the words that it says to me
I don't know if they're true but they
set me free
totally.
I don't wanna make an enemy,
I just wanna recover
I can't find it within me to
care one way or another
Adults chasing childhood like
misfortune chasing its first high,
or sex fiends desperately seeking to
relive the massacre of their virginity
These are the words that it says to me
I wake and sleep and have an awful day
and have a great day and freak
I'll find the solution, forget it all
and twenty minutes passed by quick
No I don't need anyone against me
These are the thoughts that come through me
I choose all the words and set myself free
Are you with me on this?

(continued)
These songs play in my head
in situations like these
and help me remember them even more fondly
But if I should fall into one of their traps
Where I lose my own pace taking logical steps
I'll escape from the meaning
With just enough feeling
To burst right out of my chest
These are the words that it says to me
I don't need another enemy
I know you'll make a good friend to me

WORDS *so* SHARP
Between the start of cutting your teeth
and making it work in the end,
I ache to make my words so sharp
they're painless going in.
Thrown back so quick your head'll spin,
Instant dizziness from the zing.
I can't allow my brain to rest
'til I'm right where I want to be.

...My only static occupation is Man,
and I'm not even sure that I'm there yet.

WING CAP (UPON *the* GROWING HILL)

It's like a wing cap,
closing my eyes, toward a cloud out of a cannon.

Closing my eyes…

I was on top of the hill I grew up on,
a couple jumps from the midday, post-French toast
imagination session and instead of landing, I'm
crawling through invisible nets of the scents of
childhood, some twenty feet up.

Clean laundry and chimney smoke.

"I'm going to make a couple passes really quick,"
around the tree that stood long as long as I have times
three, and how many times it's acted as a home base
cannot be tallied.

Something familiar, and it's still standing.

I can't tell you how many years it's been living
dead.

Three times circled, before we visit every single
layer of paint splashed upon century-old brick, tales of
gaudy design trends and shoddy workmanship within.

From green to brown, just like the living dead.

Secret tractor routes between walk and wall, and
busy like critter-forged midnight paths, unkempt,
unintended, just the way we like it.

(continued)

   Ignored by the neighborhood adults, they don't need to know nothin'. Secret forts and huts in shrubs, two decades now gone, but visible below the flight of the wing cap.

   The layout's lawn in filthy glory,
   told twenty years a backyard story.

F O U N T A I N
   It's raining today
   like fountains
   in Wilson Pond
   shed down quite sad
   it looks to me,
   regardless.
   I remember
   headed swings,
   like rocking horses,
   every creak with
   rising strain,
   like pendulums,
   inside the clock that
   brings back time,
   Grandfather sings.

LIGHTHEARTED *in* DEPTH

Lighthearted, in depth,
and in tune with what's going on,
I love to sit around with nothing on mind,
hitting switches,
my brain's always on.
Running laps, for better or worse,
I know somehow I'll see some sort
of benefit from the exercise.
I'm keeping my lighthearted rate up,
as in depth as it may be unwise.

PRELUDE *in* CHAINS

The entire point is to see the subtext;
The words are nothing but a vehicle
assigned in the aftermoment.
Trained to operate dysfunctional machinery.
In order to progress, we need to see
beyond;
What's sitting there in front of us
is only half of what we need.

W K N Z

Transmitting by way of smoke signal,
signature sign on quite new school,
but don't say that to him,
he don't wanna know nothin'!
Four hundred milligrams deep
at sunrise, just to start
the broadcast day,
double that by
ten after ten,
and several seconds behind
like network news.

(What would the real station say?
Would they say it in Dutch?
Could Cleo translate?)

the MORNING JOINT

Sparkled finish or filthy floor,
"How can I be expected to perform my best,
when I couldn't get some rest,
because my mind is such a mess?"
I'll start today with what I woke up with,
and add a little more of what I
never knew I was missing.

"Pilot to bombardier!"

THAT'S *the* GUY

Sometimes I write,
and sometimes I fight
with myself, do they do it not knowing,
or possessing credentials of spite?
I don't understand all the trouble it brings
and what puts the wrong in the right;
"I hope you enjoyed the performance put on,
And I hope that you have a good night.."
Sometimes, I like going to see all those
that inspire to get me to move,
And I'm not sure why they end up the ones
left to deal with what I have to prove.
"See you tomorrow, guy,"
and your name that escapes me
will somehow return to mind
when I see all the pictures,
all the ones I took with you,
and I realize that you were the guy.

SPEECH

I'll speak with my rifle,
I have since grade nine;
There are many more like it,
but this one is mine.
Rotary silence
too hot to the touch;
The sound as my ammo,
the rifle my crutch.
I speak with an axe,
swung wild but tame;
The whip of return
with noise just the same.
...I'll speak with the crevices between words
and the cracks that blemish our speech,
and I'll steal the sound
to return a feeling
our primitive letters
couldn't reach.

A . S . M . R .

"Still, I call it magic,"
sings the lyrics, infinitely on repeat,
as a same old talked-about feeling
starts to paint its world onto me.
I am in hot water now;
I'm not really sure how to explain it,
like talking viewpoints with the blind.
I couldn't explain all my playlists
on YouTube to friends if I tried...
Under influence of a low vibration,
or high like the hum of a muted television.
Wave your hands like antennas all you want,
bringing a spell of sweet sleep to the front...

CORNERS

I like to keep the corners
of the pages to myself,
my own stomping ground of
footnotes, and reminders,
and night lights, and rambling
poison crumbs.
The notebook is less and less
mine as I lose myself in it,
but I'll always come back
to my corner, and hide in all the*

EMERALD FUSION

I'm a new man,
like Sullivan
was a devil.
Slowest burn of
booking, with an
aim perfected sell.
Guidance is distracted
while I trust myself
for once,
*"Period, point black,
match, set, done."*

THE WALL

Roger Waters had his Wall,
with Dave on top,
guitar and all.
Thank the Lord he didn't fall,
and cue an early curtain call.
"Damn that Roger, all his gall
'n surr'gate band beneath it all..."

SETTING *the* STAGE

"I'm setting the stage
for talks to take place.
We'll serve 'em with
handshakes 'n
brainwaves on plates..."

BREAKING KAYFABE

There's a reason the fourth wall
has no guard rail, and how can you
ambush them if your
music is playing?

LINDEN

*asterisks.

REAL ESTATE

I've lived a cramped
and quiet life,
and money let me be;
But if I moved
across the street,
Lord knows just
what I'd be.

CXXXVI

136 is where I like to sit,
parkside fireworks and
tethered beach blankets;
Bumper to bumper
at any ridiculous time that you like,
just sitting at 136.
On a floor, mostly mine,
cross of the legs
and a spark of the flame.
Single turn from 136, so incredibly
bored and sitting content.
136 to 117, roughly a mile a number,
professionals inhale so much, what
with someone to count down with.
Someone to count it all down with,
starting at home,
doing it all,
not doing much at all,
just kind of sitting at 136...

CXVII

136 to 117, heading south on 1 and 9,
from 9 to 35, limit 40, 65,
35 eventually becomes Route 36,
just another place I like to
go sometimes and sit.

FLIP SIDE

running a business,
like running a life:
running a tab,
running a gauntlet.
all the things you have
that you need to deal with;
everything you want
to forget,
all it is that you need
to get it through your head,
and everything you give,
just to have to take back later.
a little part of that giving
is just a little bit of magic,
to make it on your own
with your own unique brand
of witchcraft in tow.
small price to pay,
tuition fees excluded.

SKYDIVING RETREAT

Embracing it like you're halfway
through a skydive;
At the same time I learned that
sometimes no action is perfect,
I realized my best was
up front all along.
I realized my rest was real,
and so are my limits,
and so are my responsibilities.
Being a friend will trump
exaggerated self-discipline;
You'll be stuck at step one,
as long as you're aware of something.

NORTHEAST CORRIDOR

Almost like you're inside a giant toaster oven,
warmed up through and through in an orange
tunnel with no reception, emerging into a place
you ain't thought about one bit. Reinforced
beauty to a New Jersey nobody.

ATTIC

Folded sheets like origami
sensed in mind and felt in body
written plans from dreams upon me
flattened streets in foreign countries.
We don't approve the blueprints of
the homes we don't inhabit, but
we can't condemn a stranger
by the records in their attic.

BIGGIE

I may be older than Biggie was
the night he passed away,
But he still makes more
money than I; What the
fuck am I doin' today?

THOUGHT GARDEN

a thought garden
with sandbox sentence structure
manifestation,
a giant sunny band of colors
across the imagination spectrum.
each word is a grain of sand
and the connection between
inspiration and action as
a little, red plastic shovel.
See-saws of conflict come in
way later,
this garden's situated deep inside
the backyard of your
playful, never-ending mind.

T H R O W *i n t h e* T O W E L

(a productive haiku)

"Finally", I sighed,
as I threw in the towel
and ran the dryer

DIGITAL BIRDS, *ongoing*
Amidst an abundance of edge and
a dissipating focus,
I come to shout at strangers in a
way transparent you can't tell
in person...
I'll smoke too many cigarettes,
and think that exercising
a brain so much
will spare a benefit, but
too much candy is bad.
All I know is what's intangible,
'til I can make it not.

FRETBOARD FINGERS

fretboard fingers,
dextral means toward
ending play of music means.
imagine fingers on
your spine,
fretboard fingers
tuned and timed.
intuition transcends art;
as playtime ends,
the work should start.
endless bout of squirm & strain
as fretboard fingers tell no pain
calloused, worn &
sometimes torn,
they train to make the
body warm.

TRUE FREAKS (LEAVE *the* LIGHT ON)

True freaks leave the light on,
pens are drawn and wet with ink,
denied of sleep;
A filthy beast on paper sheets,
bleeding all night long.

True freaks leave the light on,
pens erect and wet with ink,
dismissing sleep;
A virgin screams on paper sheets,
bleeding all night long.

PEACE TALKS

The convoluted spectrum
of paralysis by Karma
keeps you living in a cage,
be it spiritual or carnal.

The sick, depressing spectrum
of paralysis by Karma
sends a shockwave to your spine,
steals your guts and spits right on 'em.

The dreaded, evil cycle
of paralysis by Karma
takes an end when halves are friends,
Peace Talks ringing, skull to stem.

EXIT **136**
Linden
Roselle
NEXT RIGHT ↗

M U S I C A L :

"*Celestial Bodies: A 12-Month Galactic Collaboration*" (as Ruined Machines, with Michal Brodka)

One year in space allowed us to create the otherworldly audiovisual experience within. Three hours of music, dedicated to each Solar System entity and beyond, with artwork by Brodka as accompaniment. Various genres, 2012–2013. Rain Music Group.

Available for free/name-your-price at ruinedmachines.bandcamp.com.

"*Pressure & Obsession*" (as Ruined Machines)

The story of a failed rebirth, told in zero words; Only sound. Instrumental, progressive rock, 2011. Rain Music Group.

Available for free/name-your-price at ruinedmachines.bandcamp.com.

(continued)

"*Stiles 1–5*" (mini-album series, as Stiles)
Telling the tale instrumentally through the eyes of a teenage garage rock duo from New Jersey. Each tiny album represents their journal entries. 2012–2015, Third Floor Escape.
Every installment is free through the Third Floor Escape website:
thirdfloorescape.bandcamp.com

L I T E R A L :

"*Dancing To Your Own Music*"
    Sessionville.com, 2015

"*Why Did You Put Out That Awful Album?*"
  (two-part feature)
    Sessionville.com, 2013

CXXXVI